I feel caged
Confused
Dazed

I am locked away
Trapped

Darkness falls
Come upon me
Surrounds me

I am void of hope
Darkness is within me

I want to escape, but the spirit won't let me
Darkness looms
I am but a darkened soul

I feel hopeless
Lost
Defeated

I feel empty
Trapped in a world that refuses to set me free

I am caged
Dazed
Confused

I am trapped
Lonely
Empty
Void of all life.

M

Lost am I
Freedom is gone from me
I feel like an empty shell
A tree without fruits

I see the darkness
The mess of life
I see no hope
No joy

There are no stars to look to
No moon to shed a tear for you

Loneliness falls
Become your night and day
There is no light to guide your way
Just darkness
Anger, tears and pain

Hope is lost because there's no hope there
No friends
Just an empty room
Your empty shell

Hope is gone
And you're left alone in an empty room; space.

M

My mind has become my jail cell
Prison
Cage
Caged walls

My thoughts are dark
Void of light
Without stars

I am but an empty vessel trapped in a sea of no return; a sea that's rough at least so I think.

I am confused
No, not confused
Just lonely
Ill equipped when it comes to life and the confines of life.

I am my own worst enemy because life keeps throwing me lemons and I cannot make lemonade with them. How daft can I be?

It's like the internet; I cannot navigate my way through the social mediums that are available out there. I've locked myself in a world where the old suits me just fine; only to find the world passing me by at a rapid rate of speed. Go figure.

Am I willing to change this and learn?
No, I truly dislike technology. Too impersonal
Carefree

Lacking privacy

Ah technology
It can truly pass me bye
Don't need it
Don't care to have it
Don't truly want it

When all the technology has come and gone, I'll still be here writing away; still using my paper and pencil; stationary products.

Man technology
People prying in your personal life
People sending selfies of self and areas that are meant to be private.

Shit who the hell needs a good porn flick
Social media is free and people; well let it all hang out for free.

Ah life
Yes it sucks to be me.

M

Up and down go the feelings
Up and down goes my sexuality

Up and down go my thoughts
Oh damn I need a good jerk off

Frig I so need to get laid
Need me some natural sexual high

Got to get involved
Got to find me someone who truly suits me

Don't care who that person is.
No wait I do care
I am that picky

Picky me, maybe that's why I don't have a special someone.

Oh well this is me thus I live a granny life; yep that boring.

M

Take me to another place why don't you.
Take me to your world and back.

Find it in your heart to forgive me
For what I truly don't know

Just wanted to be different
Wanted to be a different me
No wait this is me

So take me to another place and back
Be good to me
Treat me nice
Truly don't cheat on me

Is my mind playing tricks on me?
Am I going crazy?

Sure looks like it because I am sexually deprived.
What the hell am I holding out for?

It's not like I am going to land me a hunky
Russian billionaire. No wait, you never know to
the way the world is going. I might just get one
don't you think. Yeah me!!!

Yes its crazy me. The coo coo one that truly loves
to blow your mind.

M

Oh man why can't I find the perfect someone to go home with?

Damn when am I going to share my bed with someone?

Do you want to share your bed with me?
Will you treat me right?
Do all the things I need you to do?

Will you be shy?
Will you be bold?

Will you be freaky?
Are you freaky?

Can you freak me my way?
Will you teach me all the freaky things you like to do?

Can I touch you my way?
Can I be a little bit rough or do you like it soft; mild, even flowed?

Will you be my forever ever baby?
Or will you be the one night stand that smash, hit it then blows?

Talk to me baby
Let me get to know you
Let me touch you

Feel you
Talk dirty to you my way

Let me turn you this way and that
Let me play, have some fun with you

Are you up to it?
Will you scream and say no?
Will you beg me for more?

No, no, no let the music play
Let me feel the rhythm while I be your misty morn

No don't take it off
Let me do that for you

Feel my touch as I make you warm.
Ah yes my chocolate pleasure
Sexual chocolate
My vitamin S

Please me baby as I please you
Let me whisper songs of love in your ears

No, no, no, no poetry tonight
You are my poetry book and I aim on making you
my guiding light.

Baby let me feel
See the juices of your pleasure
Let me touch it

Ask you questions about it

All the juicy pleasure of your juice
So thick and warm
Alive
Life

Ah my sexual chocolate you are pure pleasure
Let me look at you
Lick my lips and count the ways I am going to
make you scream out for pleasure.

My ocean is ready
Dive in
Take a swim
Enjoy the exercise; ride

Ah darling, when you are done we can go again
and again.

So are you up to it?
Are you ready to enjoy me?
Are you truly ready for the ride?

M

Oh damn I did not lock the door
Did I invite you in?

Ah yes above
The stick has come alive
So let me get on and ride your boom

Yes I'll sweep you
Clean you
Mop you

Ah the refresher
Juices overflow

Ah yes the ride
Glide
The floor

But tell me now; what kind of stick or bike are you?

I'm from the Carib; Caribbean and you know what they say. If you can't handle di wuk don't look wi. Caribbean women are not pushovers, so don't say you can manage and ha di stick when yu a little carriage.

Wi goh pon bike back thus di bumpa wey wi carry.

Wi nuh run from di ride

Wi look fi it
Thus if you can't handle di ride yu a goh get bun
an cheese.

Yu wi get leggo; thus when one gone another
come eene.

Harsh yes but stud 100 outdated
Viagra nuh strong enough fi mi

I maybe old and rusty, but when di rust gone
anna ole yu tonight.

No let Tanya talk fi mi
Soh listen to HANDLE THE RIDE AND BIG NINJA
BIKE by Tanya Stephens and listen to har. Im
couldn't handle im Caribbean ride.

Brap brap, John mash dung to claate thus
woman rule. Oman run tings because wi ha di
bak fi kill.

M

It is so weird but I have to ask Lovey
What is human rights to you?
What are the rights of humans to you on this earth?

Why does one race profess superiority over the next?

Why does one race create so much strive for others?

Why are they truly here on earth with us?

Where did justice go?
Why is there no true justice here on earth?

Why do we even seek your favour Lovey when we as humans do not favour each other, nor do we live good and right; true amongst and or with each other?

Lovey, why is one race treated worse than caged animals' whist another slaughter their character and say they are the preferred race; superior to all other races?

Why let them cage us?
Dishonour us in this way?

Michelle

I see hell
The containment of hell
The fire of hell

I see Satan
I see his people
Children

I see humanity
The cages that surround the different races

I see the evils of men
The lies they tell to rob and steal all from society
and this earth.

I see and feel the pain and I truly have to ask,
why Lovey?

Why cause and or let another nation cage us?
Treat us worse than animals
Abuse us
Take our right and rights from us including you

I feel pain to know this
Pain to know that one race have and has become
the target of everyone.

I feel pain to know that my race of people based
on hue and not good deeds had to sacrifice self,
their self worth and dignity, truth and you Lovey
for the devil. Now truly look at us.

We are void
Void of all Lovey because we truly do not have
you.

I am hurt because the tears are looming; want to
come to know that we as a people lost it all.

We sell out our own without thinking of the future
of our children and loved ones including you.

How do I go on Lovey knowing that we truly did
lose you?

How do I ease the pain **TO KNOW THAT MANY**
CANNOT SEE YOU; WILL NEVER SEE YOU OR
HAVE YOU AGAIN?

How do I go on knowing that we gave you up for
naught; death?

Yes I am hurt and it pains me; truly hurt me to
know that my people gave you up for death all
around.

Now tell me Lovey, how do I truly save me and
you from this evil faith that has befallen the black
race and community on a whole globally?

Michelle

They say faith can move mountains, but I've yet to see faith move a mountain from one place to the next.

I've yet to see faith defeat evil; the evils of this earth.

I've yet to see faith bring back you Lovey in goodness and truth to this earth.

All is see is pain and hurt.
I see a caged society.
A caged system that traps you in the hell they created.

A caged system that protects the evil and evils of this earth; world.

In all I see, I see doom
War and strife
Hate

I see a people; nations divided due to religion, class, financial worth and wealth; slavery.

I see the greed of the few, thus earth is literally decaying, sinking within. She too is dying; becoming a dying planet because of the greed of men.

Michelle

The spirit is down Lovey
The spirit is down

I see so much greed and injustice and I truly have to wonder about life.

Lovey, why do you wait in vain for man; humans?

Why do you bother with us knowing the evils of man; us as humans?

I truly don't know what to think.
What should I think?
Should I continue to have hope?

I doubt you, but when it comes to true justice I truly cannot trust you on this day because of what I see and feel. I know you are not at fault but knowing this truly do not ease my hurt and pain.

I feel it for my black own Lovey.
I truly feel it for us because it truly did not have to be this way for us. We chose to end our relationship with you and it hurts. It hurts me to know that we lost you.

We lost you Lovey and it hurts. I so wanted so much more for our people; the black race on a whole.

I needed us to truly come back to you so that we could be saved, but we failed you yet again and I feel it.

Why did we have to fail you?
Why did we have to accept the offerings of death?
Why couldn't all in the black race be saved based on hue with the exception of Babylonians?

Lovey why not us; all of us?
Why let us stray Lovey?
Were you not our true beloved?

Did you not want and need us like I want and need you if not more?

Oh my beloved, the heart is weak on this day.
My life is slowly leaving me because I feel it for my black own based on hue with the exception of Babylonians because they are truly not one of us.

Michelle

Ah Lovey let me rest my head on your shoulders so that you can ease my pain and hurt.

The tears want to come and if they do, please dry them for me because I do feel the pain in my womb for my black own.

It's sad that I cannot help them.
It's sad that all of us did not want to come home to you.

Sad that billions of us chose evil over the true and good you.

Sad that we had to give up our truth and accept the devil's own.

Oh Lovey, truly help me because I am sad on this day. My happiness has and have turned into pain because not all in the black community accepted you.

Why did we have to fail you like this?
Why Lovey, why did we have to leave you; abandon you like this?

I am so hurt and lost right now to know that we sacrificed it all for naught with the devil; our evil ways.

Yes I am concerned Lovey.

I am concerned about us as a people globally.

You are also my concern Lovey.
Do you hurt like me?
Do you cry like me?

No, I should not ask you this because I know you hurt and cry just like me.

24000 years you've been waiting for us to return to you and commit to you but we could not do this. We continue accepting lies and fail you and self Lovey again and again.

Lovey, I know you cannot forgive all, but for what it's worth, forgive me and my people for the wrongs we have done you. Forgive my children also. I know it's not December 29, your day, but I do apologize for all the hurt and pain my black people have caused you for the more than 24000 years we've been on this earth.

I am truly sorry I could not give you back everything true and clean; pure.

Michelle

Why do I feel blacklisted Lovey?
Why does nothing go my way?

My countenance is down because I tried again with my books and failed.

Wow Lovey truly wow.
I cannot go there because in all I do, please don't make me a snob or into one. Let me continue to be down to earth and friendly.

Yes I know failure and despite me wanting to give up, my heart and mind is telling me to keep going.

But with all this said Lovey, why am I blacklisted in the physical and spiritual realm?

Why is success so hard to achieve?

Failure comes quickly; in an instant, but success seems like it will never come why?

Michelle

Thank you for the warm weather this month Lovey. I am doing my best to make the best of it.

Tomorrow I am gone again providing the weather is nice and not cold or rainy.

I have to press on despite my failure today.
I have to move on despite my tears and feeling the hardship of wanting good for self and can't achieving it.

I feel so defeated in my trying.
Lovey why can't I have it easy for a change?
Why must my trying come with failure and tears all the time?

Am I destined for failure?

Yes I am grieving because for once I would like to get life truly easy and laid back.

I truly do not want to struggle anymore.

I need my life to be honest and fair; true.

Michelle

We all make choices in our lives.
We choose whether to live or die.
We choose to give up life to death for different reasons and it matters not if your reasoning is health, wealth and or financial, the hardships and pain you have to deal with in your personal life.

You feel your life is tiring.
You can't make it.
Failure is all around you.
You are locked away spiritually from finding happiness and your way in life.

You try to do right for you but in all you do, you've failed.

Depression come because you have to do all on your own. You can't go on at times because you're not strong enough.

You are lonely.
Confused.

So you give up never to live again.

Michelle

There are no apologies in life or with life just confusion and death.

Death snatches you away from life.
Death takes you to their world and drive you more insane. This is life I guess living in a world void of peace and tranquility.

Yes, I've made the conscious decision to willingly walk away from Lovey; God again. But can I really and truly knowing what is out there waiting for me in the spiritual realm?

Lord have mercy, the demons of hell would be singing and dancing saying we did it, we got her now. She's on our turf and we are going to make her pay worse than everyone here in hell combined. She knew the truth and willingly walked away from it. She knew our game and instead of being patient, she let us drive her off the path of truth to join us. She's ours and we are going to make her regret leaving the truth.

We are going to punish her more than day in and day out. We are going to make her bawl worse than a bitch in heat. Everything we will do to her. We are going to take all from her and make her an example of what you should not do or become. **_If you are on the path of truth, say on it because we; the negative forces of hell is only for a time._** *After our time is done, you are* *free to live without us bothering you. **We have to test you in order to break you. We have to inflict pain on you to see if you are truly worthy of truth.** Yes many fail because they were not strong enough, nor were they worthy of the truth. But she, she was strong. She just did not know her strength; thus she failed self and truth, and now we have her. Glory Allelujah we have her and we are going to truly eat and burn her flesh here in hell with us. We are going to make sure the outside world smell her because she is ours to keep; she left truth to join us here in hell. And just for that, we are going to let the inhabitants of hell watch and laugh at her for her shame and disgrace. She came here knowing what we were and what we would do to her. And now her payment will be severe and no holds barred.*

People, wow because I've cried wolf for far too long and Lovey isn't budging with me so no, I cannot go home and I need to grow up as a woman not just physically but spiritually because I know better.

I have to get hold of myself and stop with this emotionally roller coaster bullshit. Yes it's hard when you are alone; thus I won't piss of Lovey because I truly need him to stay. I cannot give hell the victory over him; thus I am hoping he will quell my leaving yearning and let us live stable and in true harmony.

I don't know if any of you have roller coaster days like me. I have them so often that I am sick of them. So yes, I am looking at going on vacation in 2016, but not to my homeland.

I cannot be deceitful like that.

More time I want to with what's happening in my life, but I am being selfish compared to what some of you are going through.

Yes I have health woes and stress, but some people do not have food to eat or clean drinking water to drink.

Some people need shelter.

Some people can't go to the doctor.

So in many ways I am blessed despite my limitations and setbacks. And yes I am spoilt and selfish.

Michelle

Negative thoughts came hence I wrote these and I am sharing them with you. We do have a lot of negative days when things are not going our way. We do get fed up and this is perfectly fine and okay. You give in, sleep and come clean the next day. And yes, it's harder when you do not have someone to confide in. Yes talking to Lovey is there hence these many books. Plus it's not the same when Lovey does not speak to you face to face like a human. And it's not every day I want to listen to music or have people around me. I just need my quiet time with myself and my computer.

So here we go.

I've made the decision to go back home. I cannot live on false hope anymore.

I cannot live with someone that is a liar; lies.
I cannot live my life based on false hope and promises.

I can no longer wait on a train or a flight that carries me to nowhere land and leave me on my own. Truth is important to me, but when you start out with a lie; you cannot become right you will always be wrong; a lie.

In all I seek in my personal life; I've found lies, hardship and pain. I've found confusion and deceit; pain for holding on to a God that cannot *help me financially, spiritually, health wise and happiness wise. I cannot live my life like this anymore; hence I have to move on with my life and find my enjoyment and happiness of self and spirit. It's been a hard and rocky road but I truly have to let go and be on my own.*

I cannot truly care about someone who do not have my happiness and best interest at heart. So I have to leave and make life on my own for me.

The run was good but now people, you see why no one stays with life because in truth, life is truly unfair; not just.

I find no justice in life hence I cannot find true justice in God; Lovey.

You try to walk good but there is no goodness in your walking if your road is filled with thorns; thorns that cut you and cause you to bleed.

This is my life with God hence I truly have to go; willingly let him go because there is truly no enjoyment in a dead world that is surrounded by dead people.

Michelle

The spirit is down this morning and I can't seem to get out of this slump; so I truly don't care how the day progresses.

Body feels heavy hence it's taxing on the knees because they feel swollen. The right knee feels worse than the left.

Yes I truly hate the constant blah days, but this is my world of heartache and pain; depression in my book. Hence my world of cages that keep me locked in a world I truly want to escape from.

This morning (November 1, 2015) I wrote 3 pages of darkness (pages 23-25). Counting page 23 gives you 3 pages for those who are seeing differently with the math.

After I wrote these dark pages, I went back to sleep because I did not feel like doing anything, not even make breakfast. I also had a radio show that I was to do yesterday (November 5) but that did not pan out. I knew it would not because of my dream. Dreamt I was with and or living with Blair Underwood and he moved out. He took all that he could and whatever he could not take he left behind. Mind you Blair himself was not in the dream nor was his image. In the dream it's perceived as him. Listen don't bust your brain trying to figure this out because my dream world is not like an ordinary world sometimes. There is a perceived state in the dream world that many do not know about but I do. Like I said, what he did not take he left behind and this young black lady came for the rest of his things. She was going through my things and taking some of my things and I had to tell her to put them back because those were not his. People my room was messy and clothes was everywhere so I knew my venture was not going to pan out. I was to discuss my books but it's okay. I know exactly what this dream means. It had to do with Blair Underwood being a married man and we were cohabitating and or living with each other. Now you are confused and I am so going to leave things at that because like I said, I know what the dream means.

I won't get into my earlier dreams in the morning because they are vague and I truly do not want to remember them in anyway. One had to do with exercise books on a self and the other had to do with an old boss that is of Russian Jew descent. I saw his sister crying, when she saw me she was happy and she wanted to join my hands with her brothers hand because she wanted us to be together. I can't fully remember, but I was getting his books in order because his brother left the company and he had to do it all. Doing his books for him he was happy and he put 25$ Canadian on the bed for me doing his books. Wow I know.

Dreams are weird I know. So being in a rotten mood I went back to sleep after writing pages 23 – 25. People I saw the clouds in the sky and or the heavens just spewed these beautiful array of clouds. It was the most beautiful array you had ever seen. IRIDESCENT CLOUDS are beautiful, but the colours were not like colours of iridescent clouds; nor did they appear in the sky like that. The clouds were fast and fluffy like when you would squirt whip cream or mousse if that makes any sense. When I saw this, I was so amazed that I said to this Polynesian man beside me, it's the first time I am seeing this in my existence here on earth. In my nearly 50 years on earth this is the first time I am seeing this. Note there were two men in the dream but one was Polynesian and it was the Polynesian man I addressed. He couldn't believe me because it seems these cloud formations was natural to them. But before I saw this beautiful cloud formation on this island; I was with and or going around with two young guys. One white and the other had jet black hair in a ponytail I believe but don't quote me on the ponytail but jet black hair yes. I asked the one with jet black hair where he was from and he said Hawaii. So I said you are an American; Hawaiian American, American Hawaiian. I was toying with his citizenship because he said he was Hawaiian instead of American. The two gentleman was having fun in the water and out the water. The Hawaiian fellow got this tiny, not too tiny pink surf board and he was going to go into the water with it. Oh man I am missing something. Yes on the island I saw this beautiful GREEN NEON HOME WITH GREEN NEON LIGHT. The light was not fully green, it had a hint of yellow in it but it was beautiful. It was one house that was in Neon Green and the owner decorated a part of the wall with different things. So after all this happened and talking to the Hawaiian lad I saw the clouds, fluffy clouds coming in fast in the heavens or sky.

So after talking to the Polynesian man we ended up back at the neon house but somehow I was hiding and I truly cannot tell you from what. It was then I truly noticed the wall of the house. The wall was not totally finished. Half was finished and Fuck You was on the wall. Just as how I have it, it is the exact same way he had it on his wall. The guy that designed the wall had Fuck You on it with his other decorated peace. I asked him if he was mad at someone when he designed the wall. And I think he said no and he proceeded to give me an explanation. I cannot tell you the explanation because I was truly not penetrating what he was saying to me. All I know is; I was asked if I wanted to finish the wall and I said no. I think it was the Polynesian man that asked me if I wanted to finish the wall. After all that and me coming out of hiding and I truly do not know what I was hiding from, I began to walk and I saw the scarlet dirt. The dirt of the ground was not brown or black or red, it was scarlet. A type of purple, not dark purple but more light purple. All of a sudden now this brand new white SUV type vehicle that would more look like a four wheeler dirt roadster came passing by. Because the SUV was so big no other vehicle could pass or be on the road. Trust me the white SUV was big and the white man that was driving it was big. He was in I believe dark blue pants and white shirt but his ass was big; almost as big as the lady with the biggest ass and or hips.

So, I am left to wonder because something is truly not right with me. I am so not worried about these dreams that I got a little while ago because like I told Lovey, I truly have to go because I am truly not happy with him, nor am I happy with the way my life is going.

I truly need to find me and be happy. I know he does not want me to go home and I keep leaving him but he keeps holding on to me. I need to be free because health wise I am dying slowly and before I die here on earth, I truly want to know what true happiness and true friendship and true love is all about. I had this in my mother and still do. I have this with Lovey but yet here on earth and in the spiritual realm I am truly not happy. I want and need to overcome my sicknesses. I want and need to be free of my limited space. My prosperity and progress are being hindered this I know and it's sad that Lovey is doing it. Yes his protection, but I need to be free and happy. I need my trees and waterways. I need to walk and plant trees. I need to bath in the rivers of waters but Lovey truly cannot see this.

I cannot hold on to darkness anymore. I need to be in the light of freedom and true happiness.

It's like I was briefly watching something about Kiribati and the sinking of the island and I truly did not care if the island sank. I am so heartless this morning that if anything happened to me I truly would not care.

*The reason why I did not care what happened to this island is because I am not with Babylonians and it's not truly because of that. **It's because of the politicians globally. Politicians that squander the wealth of their country and leave their land and people bankrupt. They leave their people so impoverished that some people think it's the right of another country to take them in and give them shelter.** You elected your corrupt officials to take your country's wealth by squandering it den yu waane tun trouble to a next country an race. Hell no, I am not for that; thus politicians globally I have no use for. **Stay in hell and die in hell with the*** *creeps and degenerates you elect into office to represent you.*

If you know a man or woman have no good will for you and your land, why the hell are you going to elect them into office and plunge you and your country into hell with them?

You as the citizens of the country is at fault. So why the hell should I give you land space and or access into my land? STAY IN YOUR CORRUPT LAND BECAUSE I TRULY DON'T WANT YOU TO COME INTO MY HOME AND LAND AND NYAM OFF MI PEOPLE DEM FOOD AN TEK WEY FROM DEM PROSPERITY AND SUCCESS.

You are not my bleeping burden or problem. If YOU HAD WANTED BETTER FOR YOURSELF AND YOUR COUNTRY; YOU WOULD ELECT CLEAN INDIVIDUALS THAT TRULY LOVE YOU AND THE COUNTRY YOU RESIDE IN TO REPRESENT YOU.

WHY ELECT DUPPY BAT AND DUPPIES THAT YOU KNOW IS GOING TO FEAST OFF YOU AND THE PROSPERITY OF YOUR COUNTRY?

WHY ELECT DUPPY AN DUPPY BAT THAT YOU KNOW ARE GOING TO PUT YOU AS A PEOPLE AND COUNTRY IN DEBT NATIONALLY.

The National Debt of your country IS A SIN.

*Don't go there because I am telling you, **YOUR COUNTRIES NATIONAL DEBT IS A SIN.***

No but buts. It is a sin and it goes on your sin record.

But it's the National Debt; this debt does not affect me you are saying.

KNOW THIS, THIS NATIONAL DEBT DO AND DOES AFFECT YOU. YOU ARE CHARGED WITH SIN FOR YOUR COUNTRIES NATIONAL DEBT.

Every individual that is a citizen or resident of that land that has a national debt is charged with sin and is held accountable for that national debt load. Well this is not fair.

It is fair because YOU ELECTED ROBBERS AND THIEVES TO GOVERN OVER YOU AND YOUR COUNTRY. So for each dollar that country owes; you the citizen owe a dollar and you cannot get away from this. You were the ones to elect these people to office. However, if you did not vote them into office then you have nothing to worry about. You did not mark X or put your name on a ballot so you cannot be charged with sin.

You were the ones to elect them to take your life and prosperity from you and the country that you live in.

So no, I worry not about wicked and evil leaders and the land and lands that are now going to sink.

If you as a person and or individual wanted better for self and land, you would have elected people to office that truly have your best interest at heart.

As for World War 3 I do not know why, but I get the feeling that his is going to happen real soon.

I do not know why I have this strong feeling of war because I truly cannot remember me seeing a massive war. ***But I got up feeling that World***

War 3 is going to begin thus Russia you are being warned because you are going to be the cause and or start of this with the bullshit you are doing.

YOU CANNOT INSTIGATE WAR UNDER THE QUIET. IT IS NOT RIGHT FOR YOU TO DO THIS BECAUSE HUMANITY DID YOU NOTHING.

PLEASE STOP BECAUSE YOU ARE THE SCAPEGOAT; WILL BE THE SCAPEGOAT IN ALL OF THIS AND IT'S NOT FAIR TO YOUR PEOPLE; THE PEOPLE OF RUSSIA.

They truly don't deserve to be massacred by the bullshit that is happening in this world. So truly let sleeping dogs lay. EVERY HUMAN BEING HAS A RIGHT TO LIFE; LIVE, AND IT'S NOT RIGHT NOR IS IT FAIR FOR ANY LEADEAR TO TAKE THAT RIGHT FROM THEM COME ON NOW.

EVERYTHING WILL POINT AND LEAD TO YOU AND THIS IS WHAT'S HAPPENING RIGHT NOW. I am not getting into your politics, but globally the citizens of this world has and have a right to live despite their choice. You cannot get caught up in the bullshit of this because your citizens will pay the price. They are paying the price as it is and you cannot let them (your citizens) continue to pay for something that true does and or do not concern them. No leader can say they truly love their land and citizens and engage in strife with others globally. Country X's problems do not concern you so leave them the fuck alone.

<u>Listen I will not overstep my boundaries, but YOU CANNOT MAKE FRIENDS WITH THE ENEMY.</u>

Look at your sanctions. Many lands side with other lands against you. It's not just your country this has happened to and you know what; let me stop because POLITICS IN NOT MY TRAIT OR FRIEND SO LET ME STEP ASIDE.

<u>War must come and it's a shame that billions are going to lose their life because LEADERS MEDDLE IN OTHER COUNTRIES AFFAIRS INSTEAD OF MINDING THEIR OWN DAMNED BUSINESS.</u>

NO HUMAN DOES THE DEVIL AND THEIR PEOPLE LIKE; THUS THE DEVIL PUT STRIFE IN THE LIVES OF BILLIONS. WE ARE SO FUCKING IGNORANT THAT WE CANNOT SEE THIS. THE MORE FIGHTING AND KILLING WE DO HERE ON EARTH IS THE FURTHER GOD GETS FROM US. HE CANNOT COME BACK TO

US BECAUSE WE CONSTANTLY DIRTY OUR SELF AND LAND.

As for the beautiful fluffy clouds that quickly formed in the sky I truly do not know what they mean and or what Lovey and or God is trying to tell me. All I know is, I am on my way out because I truly cannot cope by myself anymore.

War is coming and it's a pity that billions are going to get caught up and or lose their lives in the BULLSHIT THAT THEIR LEADERS CREATE.

Some hide behind religion without knowing that religion is fucking nonsense. Not one of us can take religion to the grave with us because there are no sections in heaven as you call it or in hell for the different religions of this earth.

Yes it's sad that you the citizen have to die; lose your life for the shit that men in high places create and do.

WHAT WAR CONCERN YOU?

WHAT?
WHAT WAR? COME ON NOW.

Think because your life is worth shit to some of these leaders; thus they take you to hell with them.

They have no respect for you thus they create war and strife wherever they go to kill you.

Not one know peace; true peace, and because they have no peace in their lives and cannot live in peace; they make your life hell on earth.

Their demons that walk with them urge them on; thus they live in misery and you the citizen of the land must live in misery with them or just like them.

WHY THE HELL SHOULD YOU LOSE YOUR LIFE AND PLACE WITH GOD; LOVEY BECAUSE OF MEN? MEN THAT CANNOT GOVERN YOU NOR CAN THEY GOVERN THE LAND THEY LIVE IN PROPERLY.

Unnu a cunnumunnu?

Unnu a ediat?

Why are you engaging in wars of men when you were specifically told, **"THOU SHALT NOT KILL?"**

Why are you allowing and letting these evil leaders condemn you and land?

WHEN THEY TAKE GOD; LOVEY FROM YOU, YOU HAVE NOTHING LEFT. TRUST ME YOU HAVE NO SAVING GRACE IN LOVEY; GOOD GOD AND ALLELUJAH. SO TRULY THINK BEFORE IT'S TOO LATE FOR YOU.

Stop living like the forsaken and live. No forsaken can live with Lovey; nor can they go through his door of goodness and praise; truth. Once you are forsaken by Lovey you are forsaken and there are no second chances for you. You are dead to him. See the story of Adam and Eve.

War kills; takes the life of all not just humans. So why are we as humans allowing our leaders to create strife with others?

When did God and or Lovey say, go out there and create strife with your next door neighbour?

Think because disobedience is a sin and humans are the disobedient ones. Hence disobedience is punishable by death.

Michelle

Wow because yesterday was a rebellious day for me in a brutal way. I have to continue with my rebellious ways because this is my way of slowly moving from Lovey; Good God and Allelujah.

I care not for my dream world anymore because I am so embracing my rebellious side. I've come to learn that, **"IF YOU DO NOT START OFF WITH SOMEONE TRUE, YOU CANNOT HAVE TRUTH IN YOUR RELATIONSHIP."**

YOU CANNOT GIVE YOUR TRUTH TO SOMEONE THAT DO NOT DESERVE YOU OR CAN HELP YOU IN LIFE.

LIFE ISN'T ABOUT LIES AND I FIND LOVEY WAS NEVER TRUE TO ME IN THE FIRST PLACE. And you know what I cannot fully blame Lovey and or Good God and Allelujah for all because it was written on the school wall, "FOR GOD SO LOVE US HE IS WORTHY TO BE PRAISED." It was not written on the school wall for God so love us true or God truly loves us. I was the one to jump the gun and gave my truth to someone; a god that truly do not deserve it. Yes this is me and I have to through these lonely and depressive doubts and I am truly sick of them. So I say Fuck Life and Fuck Death because neither of them are true.

I need freedom and truth in my life and I am so going to enjoy my life from now on. So I am off the wagon and I am going to live my life. No, not dirty but clean and my way. So I gave back Lovey and or Good God and Allelujah all and I am on my way to my truth and happiness; glory.

Listen people, IF LOVEY AND OR GOD HAD CREATED CLEAN INITIALLY OR IN THE FIRST PLACE, THE EARTH WOULD NOT BE IN THIS DISARRAY. I've told you truth cannot lie BUT IF WE ARE GIVEN LIES FROM THE GET GO, WILL WE NOT LIVE IN LIES AND DO ALL THAT IS WRONG?

When things have gotten this far for so long, how the hell can you come in and think you are going to fix things right away?

You cannot, thus I too blame Lovey, Good God and Allelujah for the mess on this earth. I truly cannot blame Death for everything because Death is doing their job. Lovey was not clean from the get go thus HE CREATED WILL AND GAVE HUMANITY WILL. HENCE WE ARE DECEIVED AND LIED TO BY WICKED AND EVIL MEN AND WOMEN INCLUDING CHILDREN HERE ON EARTH. He Lovey and She Lovey knows I will not give them right when they are wrong. Thus as humans and messengers we live in hell here on earth and there isn't a damned thing he Lovey can do about it. His Superman analogy to me is Bullshit thus as humans we are caged.

LOVEY CANNOT ADDRESS LIFE BECAUSE **TO ME,** HE'S NOT TRUE ON THIS DAY. When he starts being just then he can say something. If he was truth, he would have been truthful to us from the get go. Thus I gave my truth falsely and it's truly a shame. **_And I know people Lovey cannot go against the WILL OF MAN._** He did not take truth from us; we are the ones to take truth from ourselves due to our sins. But on my doubtful days; I have to blame him for everything, thus I tell him he's the one that is wrong with society.

Why allow unclean men to deceive like this?

Why allow filth that know not cleanliness to educate and teach humanity falsely?

Why allow them to take our lives and him Lovey from us come on now?

So it matters not to me if he leaves.

It matters not to me if I can't find him anymore.

This is my life now and I have to live it my way. I have to be happy. I cannot hold on to someone *that truly cannot help me. I cannot be hindered anymore in my life hence I leave Lovey alone. He can find someone else to do for him because I've found my way and I am out.*

I am rebelling. Listen you cannot show me that humans are to walk upright to you in the flesh but yet let evil men and women including children continue to deceive and kill the people of earth including the earth itself. This is truly not right. Thus I know the flaws and weakness of God literally.

So yes I am willingly and willfully disobeying Lovey on this day. No, truth cannot deceive, so I will not go there. I have to humble myself because I know the hurt and pain of life and I truly cannot hurt the one that I more than unconditionally love beyond end like this. Lovey is my beloved just like my mother is and I cannot hurt them or take life from them.

Lovey, there is hell and you cannot continue to let humanity suffer at the hands of the wicked come on now. It's hell here on earth and like I said, I feel WW3 is here, going to start and Russia is going to be the scapegoat for this bullshit.

You have demented and psychopathic men and women running and or governing society. And behind these demented and psychopathic men and women, you have the demons of hell telling them what to do. These demons are the ones who run the countries of the globe thus the 1% who say they run the world, but in truth don't. They are the lap dogs for someone more powerful.

So as the world; people of this world is divided in sections, so must the destruction of man come in sections.

Yes it's unfortunate that billions are going to die but like I've said time and time again, we are the ones to choose death over truth, true life.

Humans have and has made earth the cesspool of sin and because of this; death now comes on a massive scale.

Many sink holes are there and it's just a matter of time before they swallow up the earth.

We caused the damage and NOTHING WE DO CAN STOP THIS DISTRUCTION NOW. The clouds in the sky I truly do not know what they mean. So if you are a dream expert, truly figure it out and let humanity know. YOU CANNOT, NO ONE CAN AFFORD TO HIDE THE TRUTH BECAUSE

ZION FELL AND THE DEVIL DID WIN WHEN IT CAME TO HUMANS.

We as humans kept truth and or the truth of God out of our homes and lives. He Lovey required a home of me and I cannot give it to him because that house has and have been sold. Lovey now have to count his loss and move on to someone else because I am truly done. I've let him go and now walking on the other side. No, not the side of death but my side of comfort and truth; happiness. There is so much that I need to discover and I cannot discover it with him sitting on my ass and writing. I want and need to explore and I am going to do it even if I have to resort to begging in the street.

*Tried with Lovey and failed, so now I have to be the true me. I have to dance and endorse music that fills me with joy. Even if it's one song I will endorse it because there is a brighter tomorrow out there for me and you. We just have to let go the forces of evil. **Hey as Beres Hammond say, "GIVE IT ALL YOU GOT TODAY. YEAH. FOLLOW YOUR HEART GO OUT AND PLAY. YOU MIGHT NEVER FIND WHAT YOU SEEK, SO BEFORE YOUR OLD AND WEAK GIVE IT ALL YOU GOT TODAY."***

I have taste and feel the music; thus music is my escape from my mundane and boring world. No, I will not be a wild child but certain things I want and need to do, I am going to make a valiant effort to do so in 2016. And one of those something is to find my empty nest. Well the right someone to fill my bed.

OMG I went on Black People Meet.Com to see if I could find someone. No, I did not sign up for the website, just looking at the picture log that they show you. I checked out the reviews of people and shit that scared me off. I am rebelling people. So, relationship websites I am staying the hell off.

I need someone positive, clean and true in my life and I truly don't think a dating website will help me. Too damn scary for me hence I am scared shitless to try one. People, it's frigging scary and yes depressing for me when I have to resort to a dating site at my age to find a companion. Yes desperate on my part but hell loneliness and rebellion makes you do desperate things. So, absolutely no dating websites of any sorts for me; they are truly off my list of to do list and meeting people list.

My problem is I am too frigging intimidating. I have this spirit around me that says do not approach. I have a spirit that repels people for some strange reason. Friends are hard to meet and when you do meet people, the friendship is truly not true. I truly do not need friends, I need true friends. Friends are just there; acquaintances and after the acquaintance is done, the friend is gone. Who the hell needs that!!

Oh well I am a strange human being hence there is none like me I don't think.

And yes I know my rebellion is truly not rebellion because when you rebel, you can't think of the consequences. I have to because truth cannot hurt in that way.

I am being selfish because in truth, I never thought about my mother and the seeds Lovey gave to me. I never thought about their hurt and pain and that I am taking true life from them. So selfishness is truly not good.

Michelle

Oh before I go because I truly want to be done with this book. I wrote these November 04 – 05, 2015. I so want and need to write a poetry book by itself where all funds from this book go to the people and country of Kenya and maybe Russia, if not Cuba, but Kenya for sure. I truly need to do something positive and clean for Kenya right now, and despite my rebellious ways in this book I am hoping this can be done and Good God and Allelujah will open up a positive way for me to do so.

And no, I am not being rebellious with Kenya, Russia or Cuba. When I find out why I am so attached to Russia I will let you know. Like I said in another book, Russia has Babylonian roots and you can see this in their architecture. Thus the Babylonians roots in Russia run deep. So when we talk about purity of blood and or a race, no one is pure. We are all mixed up thus the lies spewed by men; historians and modern day man; humans.

So as I close this book do enjoy because I truly don't know if I want to continue writing spiritual books after this one. Maybe later on when my life if fixed and better and Good God and Allelujah truly come clean.

Michelle

The loneliness brings tears
There's no happiness within
Just sadness

The feet are taking me places
I leave out the apartment now
But sadness; sadness comes running back and hugging me.

Sadness missed me
Sadness cannot do without me
Sadness keeps me lonely
Trapped
Caged
Down trodden

I am alone once again
No intimacy
Just thought

No friends to call
No one to go for a coffee with

It's just me in this lonely world that I call hell; my hell.

Michelle

Wow, what a world I am living in
No wonder people go crazy
Have crazy and suicidal thoughts

What is happiness?
True happiness

What is life if you are constantly lonely?
What is life with a yoyo state of mind; emotions?

I don't know but am I to be lonely all the days of
my life?

Am I to wonder about happiness?
Why crave happiness and truth if you can't get it?

Why live a miserable existence here on earth?

Why bother think of life if all you have in your life
is loneliness; unhappiness?

No, this isn't death talking or thinking. But why
bother think of life at all? Should we not do life;
live life? But how can you live life if you are
caged; being kept from your true happiness?

Michelle

I need to break free from this apartment before I snap; literally go crazy.

The friends are coming more and more and I truly want to leave. Going for a walk helps but what the hell good does it do if you are coming back to your child's friends.

I need fucking peace and solitude not his fucking friends here every day.

I have not true peace hence I have to escape and move far away from my kids them.

I need to be free
I need to be free

I can't take the constant in and out.

I can't deal with people that feel like they have to be at my house each and every day or when they feel like coming here they just come.

I have no damned privacy and I can't take the noise.

Yes I want to snap, but before I do this; I am going to live with my niece temporarily. Yes I am going to give up my apartment for 2016.

I truly can't deal with my children.

Not all but the one that feel it's okay to constantly have people in my home.

I've spoken to my son.

I've spoken to him to limit the time this particular friend come into my home.

My spirit wanted to vomit and I told him of this but he refuses to listen. Plus schooling for the last one is an issue. So since there is no ambition there on their part and for my health and sanity, I have to go and live in true peace. I cannot provide for them anymore. Thus they are truly on their own come February 2016.

Michelle

Life sucks raising these lassa day's generation.

Life sucks raising children on your own.

Life sucks when you don't have it.
Life sucks when you are on your own.

Life sucks
Life sucks
Life sucks

My life is too lonely.
This life sucks and it hurts.

There is absolutely nothing to look at.
Nothing to see
Just a concrete jungle that takes away the
natural beauty of earth.

Earth is ruined
Humans suck
They destroy and kill natural beauty.

Michelle

What an unfaithful day
Yes Wednesday which is today was unfaithful to
me.

Wednesday cared not for me
She showed me no mercy
Couldn't care less about my success

Thursday you are my hope
Friday and Saturday you are my joy

Sunday you are my rest and hiding place.

So, Thursday, Friday, Saturday; I am depending
on all of you to bring me true joy and happiness
and an abundance of prosperity.

Thursday, Friday, Saturday truly do not
disappoint me but favour me always. Hold me up
and truly help me.

Tuesday I can't forget about you.

Monday truly thank you. And as the days turn
into night, let true goodness, happiness, good
prosperity and an abundance of wealth and
strength travel with me and surround me always.

Michelle

Lovey, I am reading the mistakes in one of my books and correcting them in my dream world because the wording makes no sense; words are missing thus the spelling of words are incorrect. But Lovey I am so lazy and I truly don't want to re – read my books to catch spelling mistakes I've missed.

Hopefully my readers can point them out and I can correct them at a later date.

See you are my editor. No, I'll go over my last two books I uploaded on Lulu and see where the errors are myself because this is truly what you want.

As for the white man that is going to attack me with a long knife who is he?

Yes I know the anger that will flare but violence Lovey come on now.

No, he did not cut me with the knife because I held his hand, but really Lovey? Has religion and politics; lies and deceit taken over the lives of humans that they would kill for the lies that they've come to know and love?

But then again Lovey, why am I asking you this question when I know and you know that this is the way humans are? They kill for a place in hell.

They kill for lies; hence the truth must not be known.

The lies of men suit humanity just fine thus they are hell bound literally.

Ah the talk; conversation. I was in this long conversation with this man Lovey. Was it you because I cannot tell you what he looks like because I did not see him?

And why am I thinking he's white?

Oh well this is life I guess. My dream world was calm except for the tall white man that came after me with a knife.

Michelle

So Lovey really!!!

My bad dreams about my death and people hurting me I leave in your capable hands because I truly need justice in the spiritual and physical world.

I need life; good and true life Lovey with you and the good and good and true seeds you've given me.

I cannot worry myself about those who want to kill me in the physical and spiritual world. True life is my keep and it's true life; you that I am expecting to truly protect me.

Life is given Lovey and if humans want to throw it away it's their choice. Let it be, but protect me; truly protect me from the wicked and evil of this world and spiritual world.

Yesterday was a disappointment but today I am renewed and ready to go again.

Yes I see my own. I grieve for them but I know why they are the way they are and I cannot be bothered with them. So I am moving forward without them.

Stature plays a part for them and since I have none with them, I have to humble myself and continue to be me. And even if I had status Lovey, do not under any circumstance let me be like them. Keep me truly humble and kind; fierce in you but truly kind and down to earth.

Never let status change me to become cold and selfish; without a heart and soul.

Those that truly help me let me truly help them, but for those that ignore me; would not give me the time of day, those that treated me with anger and so forth; do not give them the time of day Lovey; nor let me give them the time of day ever.

You know them and I know them, so I leave them be because I see and know that when you are trying, no one knows you, nor do they help you.

My one good door will open one day Lovey and you have to be with me as the head of my helm and everything. You keep me going when I can't and I truly thank you.

Michelle

It's Thursday Lovey and its foggy and bleaky. It's as if it's going to rain.

I so wanted to go downtown to hand out more flyers and books.

Lovey the rest of the week was to be good to me.

Why make it rain today and take away my blessing?

Ah Lovey, you know best; so I will leave Thursday alone and hope for the best Friday and Saturday because Sunday is my day of rest.

So Lovey in all you do today, truly remember me.

Michelle

Time is winding down and I will move away from my children.

Yes I'll move far away from them.

I'll move where they cannot drive a short distance to see me.

Out of province will do me just fine; hence I am BACK TO BRITISH COLUMBIA AND OUT OF NOVA SCOTIA.

I will find true peace on day Lovey and when I do, it's me and you forever ever all over again.

Michelle

So yes another confusing book on my part emotionally. You know it's scary because billions in this world; earth will not be saved. We were the ones to give up our life to wicked and evil people. Wicked and evil that say they govern and preach, but yet take you to hell with them.

Some of you don't believe in God which is fine because no one can believe in God, you have to know God; Lovey.

Some of you will and or may say God is made up and there is no hell. But I am telling you, there is a hell. God is real and so is death hence I tell you, **"the life you live in the living; here on earth determines where you go once your spirit sheds the flesh."**

THE SPIRIT IS YOUR TRUE LIFE AND IT'S THE SPIRIT THAT MOVES ON TO GREATER LIFE AND OR DEATH.

I've told you, we were to walk upright to God but because of sin, flesh and spirit cannot go back to Lovey whole. They must be separated. The flesh has to be left behind and go back to the earth to be eaten by worms. Thus once the flesh is shed; you go to the grave and depending on your sins, some go to hell and the rest must be

thoroughly cleaned in the spiritual realm before the spirit and or your spirit moves up to Lovey.

<u>Please note that it is in the grave that many of you are given your life and death sentence; the upright and or the downward triangle. Thus it's imperative not to interlock and or join your life choice (upright triangle) with death (the downward triangle). Once you join these triangles you are telling Lovey you forfeit life and join the realms of the dead.</u>

Well Israel has the six pointed triangle and they are the Jews.

No, Israel is not truly Jewish land. Israel forfeited life long before Adam and Eve thus they carry the star of death; The Star of David and or Mogen David. **<u>The true Israelites where the original Ethiopians and they did join with death and this is why your so called holy bible or book told you Israel is no more.</u>** *Lovey do not look upon any Israelite because they were the ones to originally sell out Lovey by joining forces with death. So no Israelite can be found in the Kingdom and Abode of Lovey. There is a hatred there and like I've told you Lovey do not hate. I asked the question using hate and was shown* the answer. So for anyone to say they are Israelite tells me and Lovey they are not of him but of the death. **THEY CARRY THE REMNANTS OF DEATH, THUS THEY LIVE WITH DEATH AS THE DEAD.**

NO TRUE JEW CAN SAY THEY ARE ISRAELITE. THEY ARE BLASPHEMING IF THEY SAY THEY ARE THUS GOING AGAINST GOOD GOD AND ALLELUJAH; LOVEY. A true Jew carry the order of life and it is life they must live by.

A true Jew cannot join death no matter the pain and heartache they feel.

But you want to leave Lovey.

Yes, but not to join death or another God. My trials and tribulations I can no longer bare and this is why I want to leave him. The hurt and pain is too much and in order for me to leave, I have to willingly sin so that he Lovey can walk away from me. I need him to see my pain and say enough is enough, no more. The suffering has gone on too long and it's time for me to rescue her from the hell she's living in.

I am not a part of the society or societies of men and or man. Politicians sell you and the clergy *sell you also. Thus both have and has sealed your faith in hell with the killings and or bloodletting and shedding they've done.* **_Religion and politics go hand in hand because they both sell and maintain death. You the people of society and or this world were the sacrifice for these men and women. So because you vote for these wicked and evil men that kill under the quiet and in the open, you are going to die._**

Because you go to church and buy death, give these wicked and evil people your hard earned money to kill you, you are going to die. Your name is written in the book of death so death have to take it.

You drink the blood and eat the flesh of man; communion, and because of this sacrifice unto death, death must take you.

You cannot be saved. And do not look at the true Jew because A TRUE JEW IS NOT GOVERNED BY THE LAW AND LAWS OF MEN; THEY ARE GOVERNED BY THE LAW AND LAWS OF LIFE, LOVEY.

Like I've told you in other books, ZION FELL. So with the falling of Zion; I truly do not know what's going to

happen to the black race. We lost because despite Satan having 24000 years to deceive and kill; take humanity to hell, we also had 24000 years to make right our wrongs so that you would be saved, and none in the black community could do this; thus Zion fell, her time is expired and billions of black people must now face their true hell.

*I did tell you Satan loves the black race and hell is full of black people. Satan knew we were not a loyal race of people and all he had to do was give you a little food that contained a tat of the truth and trap you. Thus you have black churches leading the black race astray. **So based on hue; black people are the true Judas when it comes to Lovey and true life. We trust the devil and his word over the truth; thus you have so many black churches globally that dance around and praise the devil literally.***

It's November 08, 2015 and another ritual must be performed in the entertainment world. Dreamt this long table and one that looked like Inga Swenson dressed in a light green dress, Adam Levine and some other people including that Rodriguez girl was there. Do not quote me on the

Rodriguez girl from Fast and Furious, but I cannot get her out of my head so include her. They were all sitting around the table of rectangular shape and not a circle. Justin Bieber who was dressed in a black suit had this vial of another singer's stale urine in it. Trust me the urine wreaked from the dream. Justin Bieber was passing the urine around to see who would drink it. The one that looked like Inga Swenson refused; the other person beside her refused and I woke up out of my sleep. No take Inga Swenson out of the loop because I Googled her and she's not the one. Man I can't find her on Google. The girl with the dragon tattoo is similar to her but not the exact face I want or need. There's an actress in Hollyweird with red hair I believe that matches the woman in green exactly. I won't search anymore because I am tired of looking.

So, yes another satanic ritual is going to go down in Hollyweird soon; thus sealing the fate of those who are there in hell indefinitely. Fam and People I truly cannot comprehend why anyone would sell their soul for fame; money. I know many have and has performed human and animal sacrifices and many have and has sacrificed family members and colleagues to become a part of the **ABRAHAMIC ORDER OF DEATH.** *Oh just go back to your book of death and read what Abraham did to join the realms of Satan. But what you as humans fail to realize is* ***Abraham*** _**was a part of the order of death.** Abraham was a Babylonian that practiced idol worship because his Abraham's father was a IDOL WORSHIPPER. **AND FOR THE RECORD, LOVEY WOULD NOT CHANGE YOUR NAME FROM ABRAM TO ABRAHAM; THE SON OF HAM; THE PIG.** So when I hear black people telling me they are Hamite and or descendants of Ham, they are telling me **THEY ARE OF THE ORDER OF PIGS.**_

The pig is the nastiest and filthiest animal in the spiritual realm. Dear God you don't want to know just how nasty and filthy this swine is. And yes, this is why some voodoo or obeah people use pork and Aloe Vera and or Sinclebible in their voodoo or obeah rituals. Trust me this is one of the highest form of obeah and voodoo out there.

Further, I do not comprehend how many blacks can they praise and worship including sing for Lovey when many are Masons; of the Masonic Order of Death.

So now I ask you, whose going to save them?

Who is going to give them a saving grace?

So all around death and or humans have and has sacrificed self and family to hell. Thus Bob Marley told you, **"NOTHING CAN STOP THEM NOW."**

We cannot stop death because death own earth and the people of earth. Well not Lovey's children the true Jews.

Can a Jew, true Jew rescind the contract of death?

If they are ordained, yes. Thus you as a chosen messenger is a threat to death and you are killed. And I am not contradicting myself to what I've told you. True messengers can save you, but as for me, I will not save wicked and evil people; nor will I save people that willingly and willfully give their soul to the devil for money and fame if I am the saving grace of humanity. **YOU KNEW THE CONTENTS OF THE CONTRACT AND YOU SACRIFICED SELF AND FAMILY INCLUDING FRIENDS FOR MONEY.** *And in truth I am hoping that Lovey makes it forbidden as of December, December 2015 to save anyone that has and have sold their soul for money, fame and or what have you more than forever ever without end.*

It all comes back to us people. We are the ones to give our soul over to people that has not our best interest at heart. **THEIR SOLE AND OR SOUL PURPOSE WAS TO TAKE YOU TO HELL. YOU WERE THEIR SACRIFICE AND THEY DID SACRIFICE YOU FOR PROPHET WHOOPS PROFIT.**

Your life and existence on the face of this planet meant nothing to them. They got what they wanted from Evil so they bask in their greed; riches, without knowing that they too are going to die. They sealed your faith in hell without knowing their fate is sealed in hell also. Ole people sey when yu a dig ole, dig two and they were so right.

THEY KNEW THE MORE YOU SIN IT'S THE FURTHER GOD AND OR LOVEY GET FROM YOU.

OUR SINS LOCKED LOVEY OUT OF THIS EARTH; THUS NULLIFYING YOUR SAVING GRACE WITH HIM.

Lovey cannot come into a dirty planet and because of this, he chooses messengers that would help him. But as time went on, many messengers joined forces with death; sold out for money and the luxuries of this earth. Thus giving rise to death and the nastiness of hell here on earth.

What these people who have sold their soul and or spirit to death don't realize is that; THEY OWN NOTHING. ANY CHILDREN THEY HAVE AND OR THAT IS BORN TO THEM

BELONG TO DEATH; THE DEVIL AND OR SATAN. They are slaves and they have to do whatever their puppet master say.

And it matters not if you adopt a black child. That black child cannot save you; they're just your black sacrifice unto your god and gods.

BLACK LIVES MATTERS NOT TO MANY OF YOU, THUS BLACK BABIES WERE FED TO GATORS BY SOME OF YOUR WHITE ANCESTORS OF OLD.

MANY BLACKS WERE MURDERED; KILLED BY SOME OF YOUR GERMAN, ITALIAN, GREEK, BABYLONIAN, SPANISH, FRENCH AND ENGLIGH ANCESTORS. So no matter how you look at it; BLACK LIVES MATTERS NOT. We the black race do not matter because we are not unified nor can we unify with each other. *We are so divided that Bob Marley had to tell us,* ***"WHAT WE KNOW IS JUST WHAT THEY TELL US"*** *AND HE IS SO CORRECT.*

MARCUS GARVEY HAD TO TELL US, "A PEOPLE WITHOUT KNOWLEDGE OF THEIR ROOTS ARE LIKE TREES WITHOUT ROOTS," MEANING, WE ARE DEAD AND HE IS SO CORRECT. The black race is so dead that we cannot accept the truth of our self. Some of us bleach our skin to look white *and feel white without knowing that no matter what you do to erase your black skin, you're hating self. You belong to the group of self haters that cannot see the true beauty of self; your spirit within. So because of this, you accept death in the living and you have absolutely no place in the kingdom and or abode of Lovey. You accepted true death in the living so you must go directly to hell and burn. You relinquished your right and rights to Lovey because **the foundation of all life is black not white;** thus you gave up life all around. And now I will say this again, **"the life you live in the living, determines where you go once the spirit sheds the flesh."***

YOUR BLACK OR WHITE SKIN DOES NOT MAKE YOU THE PERSON; IT'S YOUR GOODNESS WITHIN THAT SHAPES YOU AND MAKE YOU TRULY BEAUTIFUL.

So no matter how you change self, you cannot change your spirit; your true DNA.

When you are of the order of death, you do not control your life. You have no life because you are dictated to. Hence you live under and with dictators that pick and choose who you marry, who you sleep with, who you befriend, and what drugs you take. You have to sell the nastiness of sin; hell, like open marriages, promiscuity and whoredom. You become the whore and prostitute of the hierarchy that run the satanic organization you are a part of. Thus in all you do, you sell death and hell thus contributing to keeping truth; Lovey from coming back to earth. Your spirit is truly not yours because you did sign a legal and binding contract with death.

All is controlled thus the money you make is truly not yours. You are using the devil's money and when the devil has no use for you, he spits you out like a rag doll and make you act the fool. You go back to the bottom of the food chain until when they are ready for you again they give you another chance to redeem yourself with them (death). You do not know that **YOU CAN NEVER BE REDEEMED IN LIFE. YOU GAVE UP LIFE THUS DEATH CONTROLS YOUR EVERY MOVE. SOME OF YOU ARE KILLED BECAUSE YOU ARE USED AS A SACRIFICE AND YOUR CHILDREN HAVE TO TURN PROSTITUTES FOR THE PEDOPHILES THAT ARE HIGH UP IN THE ORGANIZATION.**

Oh before I go, dreamt I was in LA again and I was at this gas station. Man the cars were different because they were more like trucks made of steel. I saw this one black girl gassing up this truck and she let the gas overflow. The truck had two compartments for gas and I said, you have two gas compartments and she said yes. All in all gas was being wasted. I was with my brother at the gas station and he came back from paying for gas I guess. I was about to go into his car, but this white man went into the driver's seat so my brother could not take me where I had to go. My brother said to me, get some clothes and the white man who was chubby drove off and I remembered my brother did not give me any money to buy clothes. The chubby white man said don't worry he's got clothes. He pulled back the seat the reveal a pile of shirts. The top shirt being red but there was blue shirts in the pile. He drove me around LA and we came to this region where he had to meet someone. He came out the car and I followed him and he told me I could not come. He met this white man in a grey suit; did his business and he came back in the car. See the white man that was with me was a cop but he sold drugs. I asked him if he was a drug dealer and he said yes and I had to be quiet could not tell anyone. So yes I am a snitch now because I am telling the lots of you that someone in the LA Police Department is a drug runner and or drug dealer under the quiet. This white man like I said is chubby and I would peg him to be around 55 give or take a couple of years with red nose. Well big nose that is red. You know when some white men drink and or is alcoholic and you see the redness in their nose from the drinking. Well his nose was like this. And no this cop does not wear a police uniform so I would peg him to be an undercover officer. Don't quote me on the undercover. So now; there goes my credibility of being a non snitch with the police department because I am ratting one of their own out. Hey I tell you what I see and in my book, as police officers you are sworn to uphold the law and there is accountability; a form of respect that you must carry and uphold. You cannot take away the dignity of your fellow officers no matter how hard your job is. People trust you, so uphold your status of trust and not bring same to a prestigious job come on now. Uphold the law no matter how shitty your job and pay is on certain days. Bring back dignity to the police force.

I know some of you work for horrible bosses that bend the law and tell you to bend it and it's truly a shame that some of you have to do this but trust me, the hell that's going to be unleashed here on earth soon, they're going to wish they'd upheld the law themselves. All will be paid for their evils, so truly worry not about the evil ones that are on the devil's payroll.

So after him doing his business this man kept driving me around. He drove me to a school where black students went. I saw this little black boy around nine playing rough with this black girl *who was of the same age I would say. I told him he was wrong to do what he did to the little black girl and he should apologize and he did. The little girl did him something and would not accept his apology and I said that was not nice apologize. People, di likkle gyal tun pan mi an cuss out mi what not claate inna di dream. Har school uniform come off and you could see her slight oriental eyes and jet black hair whey inna a bun and har I think red, no not red, but black skirt. Wow di pickney cuss mi and I told her something like she is not going to get anywhere in life but those were not my exact words. All I knew in the dream was she was condemned; a sin. I went to the side of the building and was talking to a white female teacher and she said this was how the children behaved. I saw this little fence, kinder garden fence I call it. She said they keep building them and the kids keep tearing them down. Upon hearing that I began to help replant the fence and I woke up out of my sleep.*

Do not think a fence fence when I say fence. You know those garden fence they use. Oh never mind, I am going to Google to see if I can find the fence I am talking about for you to see. So truly do not sue me because I use these pictures from Google for illustration purposes only.

This is the best picture I could find. Now take out the Y shaped panel inside and you have the image of the fence I am talking about. The fence was not of metal but wire that you stick in the ground. And no the panels did not join each other. They were single pieces and some were more circular that you could stick in the ground. Shave off some of the height of this panelling; a tad bit and you get the exact height. I have no clue what this dream means so I am so going to leave it alone. Di pickney cuss mi and to the behaviour of the black children; they were unruly children that did not want protection but wanted to do their own thing. So truly good luck with us as a race and people.

Like I said, Zion fell and I truly do not know what this mean on a whole for black people globally.

Like I said, I cannot fathom why anyone would want to die and go to hell and become Abdullah's; slaves to the demons of hell. As humans your spirit has no say in hell, so why let others give you false hope and false promise?

Your life is truly worth it, so why give it away falsely to those THAT ARE SACRIFICING YOU?

You are the sacrifice for the many because politicians sacrifice you to death with the evils they do behind closed doors. These politicians must kill for their place in hell and I truly do not know why. All that the devil and or wicked and evil people promised them must come to an end. Evil cannot continually reign. Something has to give and it has given; hence the harvest comes before 2032 and every human being on the face of this planet must pay according to his or her sin and sins; works and or evil deeds.

We as humans made it so because we gave these men and women control and dominance over us.

We made sin; wicked and evil men and women including children change our lives by bringing death into it.

*We were the ones to believe their lies over the truth and now nothing can stop the destruction of man. **The seas have to reclaim their own and earth is becoming the SINKING FIELDS.** Land spaces are sinking thus the craters of earth that cannot be filled. We misaligned earth's magnetic field thus shifting earth ever so slightly. Thus man cannot feel the rumbling and grumbling beneath them.*

The devil told you **WHAT THEY WERE GOING TO DO IN GENESIS AND YOU DID NOT LISTEN. YOU GOT CAUGHT UP IN IT ALL AND NOW LOOK AT IT; YOU'VE LOST YOUR LIFE LITERALLY. Now billions of you are expecting a saving grace but how can one save you when that one did not sin for you? What sin did he do for you on your behalf?**

So why should he die for you?

You sinned for self thus you must die.

And as your book of sin said, only 144 000 will be saved from the 12 twelve tribes. And truly don't quote me on this; read Revelations for yourself and get the full story. So if there is only 144 000 that is going to be saved, **WHERE IS THE REST OF YOU TRULY GOING TO GO?**

Are you all Jews?

Go ahead and say it so I can truly school you.

Absolutely no one can change the laws of life and death; not even Lovey himself, come on now.

Life and death is set and no one can change the record of them. No one can include wicked and evil people into life and death. Wicked people have time to do their evils but good hath no time. Thus you were told, **'THE WAGES (PAY) OF SIN IS DEATH.** *No one can redeem you of your sins except for you. I can't nor can Lovey because Lovey told none of us to sin. He Lovey gave us Will and we were the ones to dirty Will by choosing evil over good. Yes I can help you by telling Lovey to share my goodness with you if you are clean; one of his, but I cannot share my goodness with you if you are not a part of the true banner of life.*

Like I said in another book, there is over 7 billion people here on earth and if only 144 000 of you that are going to be saved, what say the rest of you?

Who is going to speak for you and save you?

Some of you are banking on the black child and or Black Jesus, but what many of you truly do not know is; **NOT ALL BLACKS ARE OF GOD; GOOD GOD AND ALLELUJAH, LOVEY.** *So the black bank for many of you is empty* **BECAUSE ZION DID FAIL; FALL, AND HER TIME HAS AND HAVE RUN OUT.** *Once again, Black People did not choose truth, thus; truth have to go back home and truly leave them alone.*

We did not want saving so we continually neglect our calling and fail.

We could not see the bigger picture and truth. **Satan won over man and there isn't a damn thing humanity can do about it.**

Well I go to church. Koodles to you because **YOU WERE BOUGHT AND SOLD BY THE CLERGY; HENCE THEY TELL YOU ABOUT PROFITS WHOOPS PROPHETS.**

You were the prophet's whoops profit of the clergy because THEY GAINED YOUR SOUL AND SEALED YOUR FAITH IN HELL LITERALLY.

Don't with the but buts and lies. You have no soul because you desecrate the homes you say are of God with your filth and nastiness.

YOU PUT MEN AND WOMEN ABOVE LOVEY; THE GOD YOU CLAIM TO SERVE AND LOVE. Yes love; thus you HATE, BECAUSE LOVE IS HATE and TRUE LOVE IS TRULY RARE.

Don't say it because it's the ones that say they love you that leave your ass at the altar of death.

It's the ones that say they love you that kill you.

It's the ones that say they love you that screw around on you and bring home their diseases of nastiness to you.

Some of you are living with AIDS AND HIV, Syphilis, Chlamydia, Genital Herpes, Genital Lice and or Louse.

You name it you are living with it because of LOVE.

It's the ones that say they love you that; take your hard earned money and support other women and men whilst neglecting you and your children.

It's the ones that say they love you that; leave you struggling financially whilst another man's child and or children is well fed and yours go hungry because every pay cheque they get, they take it to feed another and neglect his or her family needs; own.

It's the ones that say they love you that sell you to death for a place with death in hell. Hence the human and animal sacrifices some of you do on the down low. Not to mention the shit that some of you have to accept for the dollar bill. You've become slaves to the higher up. Thus the other form of slavery that humanity truly don't know about. Slavery that you have to go through to be on top because you have to ride the devil's broom stick each and every day lest you are killed.

So because of this, and the devil knowing the weakness of men and women; these men in high place create laws to suit them. Laws that you have to live by because they say so.

Laws that take away your basic right and rights to life; dignity. They own you and there isn't a damned thing you can do about it because they have your signature and blood written on their demonic contract (s).

So as humans, we cannot blame all on the devil because we are the ones to want what the devil has without seeing the beauty of self; you.

Some of you want a bigger ass, bigger boobs, a different nose, lighter skin; YOUR IDEAL OF WHAT MAN SAY IS PERFECT WITHOUT KNOWING THAT YOU ARE PERFECT FOR YOU. Hence Solomon told you about vanity and how vanity IS A SIN PUNISHABLE BY DEATH; THE DEATH OF SELF AND SPIRIT.

And no, it matters not how death gets paid as long as death gets paid. **Politicians have to kill for death and it matters not if it's a plane or building filled with people coming down. The**

bottom line is, you the people of society are their sacrifice. You must die to satisfy death and there isn't a damned thing you can do about it because you elected these men and women into office.

Initiations do happen hence some planes do not go down just like that. The killing spree must continue because shortly there will not be any land space for humans to drill; rape of its resources. Population control is a must and at the end of the day, if you cannot pay then you must die.

Hurricanes come and go.

Tornadoes come and go but at the end of the day, drought stays. Rainfall is minimal in some lands; thus your crops will feel it and you will feel it in your belly and pocket books real soon.

DEATH WAS WHAT HUMANS CRIED FOR AND BEGGED FOR, AND ITS DEATH THAT YOU WILL NOW GET.

Michelle

I don't know people. This morning November 10th I had some odd dreams. I dreamt this young black boy. He was sleeping with this married woman. It's weird because I was creating a love story in my head. I often do this to get me to sleep. Man if I could jot these love stories down that I create in my head, I would have a quarter library of books if not more.

*So creating the love story in my head, I fell asleep and was brought into this dream with the young black boy that was having an affair with this woman. In the dream he had 3 brothers and all four of them was in a picture and I saw the picture. Apparently all four boys had died in a fire and this young man that was sleeping with this woman was a ghost. But in the dream, you would not believe he was dead. He did not fit the profile of a dead person and he seemed alive. **Just know that the dead can make themselves seem as if they are alive. I can't explain it but know that the dead; evil dead can do this and some do do this.** So, somewhere in the living this dead person is sleeping with someone in the living; the dead is interfering with someone sexually. I cannot tell you the country it is happening in, but know someone is being interfered with. So if you know someone that has had their children died in a fire somewhere and the eldest one was in a relationship with* *someone, please tell her to guard herself because death is interfering with her sexually.*

I also dreamt this very dark black man. He reminded me of Future Fambo.

Think round face and height people and nothing else. Like I said, he was very dark and he was flossing because he had money. I can't remember if this one particular guy was a part of his crew, but all you saw was this dark man tossing change on the young man as if he was some kind of garbage. Thus I cannot comprehend why we as black people have to show off anna smell wi self when wi get a likkle money. We disrespect our own like money a everything. Thus ole people sey, di higha di monkey climb a di more dem expose.

Wi guane too damn highty tighty. Thus show off cannot see when dem a goh fall.

Also dreamt I was reading that a storm was brewing and it hit Jamaica. You know what people; I am so not going to put any emphasis on this storm because I am so tired of the Jamaica destruction dreams. It's been years now I am dreaming about Jamaica being destroyed an di lan or country caane destroy yet. So I am so going to toss this dream in the garbage heap and watch with one eye open sort a speak.

I know I had another dream but I am so going to leave it because my home this morning was truly not right. Too much spirit interference and I am so going to leave this alone because I know when duppy inna mi apartment. These are the days when you need someone beside you for real.

Sometimes you get tired of them.

*Oh I went to the doctor and I met this lady; Mrs. Green, Odette Green. People, no, young children and children, **I AM TALKING TO YOU NOW.***

KNOW THAT THERE IS A HELL AND THERE IS NO ESCAPING YOUR HELL IF YOU MISTREAT YOUR PARENTS.

Bad blessings do fall upon you and when you grow older, bad blessings is going to fall on your children if you decide to have children. There is no escaping this.

LISTEN TO ME AND LISTEN CAREFULLY. THERE IS ABSOLUTELY NO FORGIVENESS IN THE GRAVE. SO IF YOUR PARENTS OR PARENT IS GOOD TO YOU, TREAT THEM GOOD. NEVER DISRESPECT THEM FOR A WOMAN OR A MAN.

Yes tongue an teeth do meet with parents and sometimes well a lot of times I go off on Lovey. But despite the arguments we have and my harsh venting on him and with him, I do truly love him more than unconditionally.

ABSOLUTELY NO ONE ON THE FACE OF THIS PLANET OR UNIVERSE WHETHER LIVING OR DEAD CAN TELL ME TO DISRESPECT HIM AND LEAVE HIM. HELL BC TUN UP BECAUSE IF YOU THINK A SAFETY ON YOUR PART; A SUDDEN DESTRUCTION.

Yes I tell him I want to leave him but di day yu cum sey Lovey dis or dat yu betta tek di uttermost part of the BC universe and not let me get to yu or find you. Di badwud dem wey mi a goh tell yu, di demons of hell curl up inna caana. My mom wuss; thus Lovey gets jealous of our relationship at times.

No one can tell me anything about my mother thus she is saved because I know what she did for me in the living and in death.

Lovey and my mother are my special someone and no one disrespect them or try to take me from them. So if you have a good mother and father that is there for you, protect you, shelters you and counsel you in a good way; never ever let anyone disrespect them or take them from you.

Do not take yourself from them. And it's matters not if he or she is not your biological parent or parents. As long as they are treating you right and as one of their own, truly love them because at the end of the day, they are your parents because they did own you as one of their own. Never disrespect truth and true love. **I know Lovey is my father, but he's my truth and true friend also; thus our yoyo relationship. As a friend and confidant I take out my frustrations on him. HE DOES LISTEN. TRUST ME HE DOES. WHEN I STEP OUT OF LINE HE LOVEY PUTS ME IN CHECK AND YOU SEE THIS IN SOME OF THESE BOOKS. So don't think he's not there because he truly is. He's your guide and rescue, so truly learn to be truthful to him. Also, have a true and good relationship with him.**

NEVER EVER LET A SKIRT OR SHIRT TELL YOU TO DISRESPECT THEM; YOUR PARENT OR PARENTS. PUSSY AND DICK IS A PASSING FANCY THUS SEX SHOPS ARE THERE.

Any woman or man tell you to cuss your mother or father or both; RUN DEM BC FROM YOU. NO DICK OR FRONT IS WORTH YOU LOSING YOUR SOUL FOR. *Keep your good parents close to you at all times because they are* *your saving grace. They give you good counsel so learn and keep the good counsel they give you.*

The reason why I am telling you this is because I met Mrs. Green today and she told me about what she is facing in her life. What her husband and children did to her and tears came to my eyes. Man did she ever tell me about our black own. I know some did wicked, but man, a soh wi wicked an tan?

A soh wi dreadful that we do not think of life after the shedding of flesh in the grave?

A soh wi love hell dat wi affi gi up wi soul an spirit to di dead of hell?

Wow, some a wi a truly BC crasses inna di living to Yass. BC man, a soh wi fucking wicked and disgusting to wi owna flesh an blood?

A soh wi fucking jealous?

Bumbo red man, a soh wi tan inna disya day an time? Wow.

No, di jealousy and wickedness do not surprise me, but when you hear pickney soh wicked to di madda wey birth dem; den mi haffi BC cry out to yass. Come on man, I feel it with my children and I know exactly who they are; what they are capable of, but to lef yu mada fi walk pan eee street penniless and homeless, man den BC fuck you because I know your BC hell and it is more than truly deserved on your part. Do not abuse your parent, especially a madda wey sacrifice fi you soh.

No man, hell not BC fair when it comes to the treatment of some of you. Death is a fucking bitch nigga in my book to di way death treat unnu. No mother should be mistreated. Murda, murda, murda. Unnu too fucking wicked hence retribution time draws nigh. Allelujah

Fucking wicked, unnu noa wey unnu du?

Unnu noa? Allelujah.
Unnu noa?

Woe murda, murda, murda. Allelujah.

Yes God, Allelujah, have mercy lord because condemnation is on the lots of you literally. Run goh beg unnu madda forgiveness. Beg har. Come on now man. Woe Allelujah, beg har forgiveness, beg har, beg har come on now.

No man should rape their wife of their dignity. When you were starting thievery did not come into play, so when front tek some a unnu claate lef di greed a door. Do not rob your wife of *everything to give to another pussy or dick. Come on now. No, right is fucking right but some a unnu man an oman fucking unfair. Thus when some oman hang unnu by the dick and take it all don't complain. Think of what you did to your spouse that you robbed and left for her; your new found Delilah.*

Black kids; children some a unnu literally fucked.

How the fuck can faada an pickney rob mother soh to BC? Fuck man, money a money and your mother cannot be replaced take that from me. A good and true mother and father can never be replaced; so cherish them while you have them here on earth. If you have a good mother, how the fuck can you let a fucking pussy; skirt turn you from your mother?

Yaa fucking ediat fi mek oman tun yu inna cunnumunu especially one mixed with Babylonian?

Truss mi, DI EYE WATA WEY UNNU MADDA SHED TUDAY, MI A TELL UNNU SEY EEE KETCH UNNU CLAATE AND THERE IS ABSOLUTELY NOTHING ANY OF YOU CAN DO TO SAVE YOURSELF AT THIS MINUTE. UNNU DONE TO CLAATE. Thus heed my cry and go beg your mother for forgiveness. Beg her for forgiveness lest your punishment take your lives.

I know my relationship with my father is not the best and I keep away from him. But fi stan up and tell him dutty badwud no. I cuss Lovey but when I go at him it's for his own good and I do not put him on a father level. I put him on a true friend level. But to say someone tell me to leave him. Not a kaka caana to BC. Take your fucking decrepit stench hole of a cesspool crap; shit and chuck literally. Give up Lovey fi who?

I know the hell I went through despite me telling him I am leaving. He was there for me and I will never forget this and this is why I stick to him so. He sent help when I needed help despite my ungrateful words sometimes. I will defend him so truly don't come around me with your god and gods including satanic bullshit. Keep death and I will stay by and keep my life; my good and true beloved, Lovey. I know money is a bitch, thus many children mistreat their parents for money.

Many rob them.

Many shove them in nursing homes, but WHAT MANY OF YOU CHILDREN DO NOT REALIZE IS THAT PAYBACK IS A BITCH AND WHEN RETRIBUTION TEK SOME A UNNU, AN UNNU GOH MAD AS CATUS CAT; DON'T SAY NOBADY OBEAH UNNU, A RETRIBUTION A TEK UNNU BC BECAUSE UNNU TOO FUCKING WICKED AND DISGUSTING TO UNNU PARENTS.

Money should not let anyone turn on their parents or parent like that. Man I felt it for Mrs. Green to know that some black children have become like this. I have it hard with my children and I can relate to her and her story of how she lived when she first arrived in Canada. My mother lived in a rooming house too and lies were told on her, but she lived to be vindicated. When you are young you don't think that you are going to get old.

You don't think the bad treatment you dish out to your parents is going to come back and haunt your ass. Thus some of you get abused in nursing homes and hospitals.

Some of you are left on the street to die and some of you do go mad anna walk up and dung road without sense.

So listen to me and know; THERE IS NO FORGIVENESS IN THE GRAVE. IF YOU'VE ERRED YOUR PARENTS OR PARENT, BEG THEM FORGIVENESS IN THE LIVING.

My God man, what have children become?

I also met this other lady from Grenada and trust me I truly don't want to get with a man again after what I heard. I've been through hell with men here on earth and in truth I am afraid of them to yass to how some a dem wicked.

This lady from Grenada went through one rough relationship and she's married again. When she told me she has to take 19 pills each day, I look at myself and say, what the bleep am I complaining about? I do not take so many. She's on pills for depression, diabetes, high blood pressure; so my complaints are nothing compared to hers.

So in all my rant and carrying on, Lovey has shown me yet again; there are people that are far worse off than me. So as I grow, I truly hope he helps me with the complaining. Mrs. Green is going through it and she is so strong. Her leg is worse than mine and shi walk strong; an shi olea dan mi. So yes I've found strength and inspiration today. Strength and inspiration I needed. Thus I remember Margaret in LA and her ordeals she faced and still facing in life. I have strong women in my life, and even if they are just passerbies, they are still there.

Also, for some of you black kids that like fi goh a people yaade an nyam, cut it out. Stop nyam, nyam a people yaade. Hence I more than over stand why some family members do not eat from restaurants and certain people. Some a unnu man fuck because pussy wata a bitch fi real. Thus the nastiness of what some women in the Caribbean do to catch man when it comes to bath water, drinking water and food.

BC nasty dem, wey tie man. And some of you men are no different because some a unnu tie oman pan unnu claate like unnu own dem. Thus the witchcraft and science including devil worship some of you men and women including children engage in; do.

So ladies and some a unnu man tu. Do not be discouraged when you hear some man sey dem a nuh bowcat; nyam aunda sheet.

Stop telling unnu oman sey unnu a goh oman wey use dem mouth fi clean unnu riffle. Some oman use dem punash fi ketch man, thus when a man tell yu sey dem naa nyam certain type a food a month time from dem oman dem noa wey dem a talk bout. Dem noa di nastiness a some oman. Some a unnu man an oman tie an nuh noa sey unnu tie.

Nastiness will never stop, thus the earth and universe you too are guilty for permitting shit like this to happen here on earth.

You Mother Earth and the Universe act powerless when it comes to evil and the evils humans do. Thus you are both guilty of not truly protecting good and true life here on earth come on now.

Michelle

So as I close this book, the dreams are getting weirder. Can't remember my dreams on the 11ᵗʰ so I am going to let it be. Truss mi, yesterday was one for the books. Had no electricity for 12+ hours but its life. Sometimes you have to face hell.

You may be walking on the right path but the devil comes along and throws you curve balls for you to lose your way.

Hence it's truly not easy when you are walking on the road of Lovey alone.

Dreamt this morning I was in Africa. I was in this tiny country where Babylonians and Blacks lived together. I was been led someplace, but to where I truly did not know. The houses were dilapidated and spacing was cramped to walk. People; the people, women and men were wrapped up. Meaning the men looked as if they were wearing mummy clothes because they were wrapped up and they had turban like wrapping on their head. The ladies were dressed in black from head to toe and you could not see their faces. They had jail cell paneling in their face covering and some had stick jail paneling. The fingers nails of the ladies were long and painted in black. It was the most disgusting sight you had ever seen. God, another day of seeing hell and their people. Suffice it to say, I did not get far because I back tracked and did not go into the center of hell. Going back I saw my own black people. This one particular black lady held on to me. She had red in her face. Not red blood or red anything, but a part of her skin was red like in blood red, no not blood red. Yes, blood red but you will not comprehend the red I am talking about. She held on to me because she thought I was a seea oman. She told me she was looking for her brother and could not find him. I put my hand on her head and said something to her and she followed me. I saw these guys and I asked them about her brother. They said they've never heard of him and or never seen him, but for me to go where these flags are. There were three (3) flags. One Jamaican Flag, One Blue Flag and the other flag had red in it. The three flags were together as if joined; cramped in the place they were put. Going through the door I saw this group of dark African men, young men. There was this older dark skinned man there that was lying down. He was a Obeah man and I said you know he's going to die. The young men could not believe what I said because they were taught to believe that the Obeah man with them could not die. They said he can't die or was not going to die. I said yes, he's going to die. People I don't know what happened next, but I ended up outside and I saw this white man dressed in pure white. It's as if he was with us but he was not. He had a small bag of cocaine in his hand and this other person, black person I believe had this big bag of cocaine and fighting broke out. They started to shoot at each other. So if you can figure this dream out please do so. But there is a drug war coming that is going to involve Caribbean and African people. This is my take, I could be wrong.

I can't remember this dream fully but it involved water and me seeing fighting. Yes this is in Africa because it's not the first time I am seeing this river. I've seen it before in my dreams.

So as I close this book truly think about you.

NEVER FORGET, LOVEY DOES NOT EXCLUDE ANYONE OUT OF HIS ABODE. WE ARE THE ONES THAT TAKE US FROM HIM AND EXCLUDE SELF OUT OF HIS KINGDOM WITH OUR SIN AND SINS.

The more we sin is the further Lovey get from us. He does leave us alone to our own will. There are no but buts.

It's time to stop excluding yourself out of his world because there is a hell, and you truly don't want to go there.

If you can amend and or make amends for your sin and sins, truly do so in the living. **No pastor and or clergy man or woman including child** *can forgive you for and or of your sins. IF THIS WAS THE CASE, NO ONE ON THE FACE OF THIS PLANET WOULD DIE. WE WOULD ALL BE LIVING AND YES WE WOULD SEE GOD AND OUR LOVED ONES. THEY (our loved ones) WOULDN'T BE DEAD, THEY WOULD STILL BE LIVING.*

No man can die to save you either.

If one man died to sake us, why do we still have to shed the flesh; skin?

If I am the son of God, I should be able to stop death and say death no more. Be gone from earth infinitely and indefinitely more than forever ever without end so that my people can truly live.

You are not needed or wanted because I am here. I am saving my good and true people in the name of God and you cannot stop me nor can you conquer me or hinder me.

I am life, a part of the true breath of life and I command you to leave my good and true people alone. Be gone from earth now I command you in the name of God, my father, Good God and Allelujah. Allelujah Glory to God.

So people know who you are giving your life to and truly stop doing it. I know some of you can't because of the contract you've signed. And in truth, it is not my place to tell you to stop doing what you're doing. Your choice is your choice so truly forgive me. Just think about you and your life and walk good and truly live. Hell is not a place for the spirit because **HELL IT WHAT SLOWLY KILLS THE SPIRIT.**

There is a price to be paid for sin and it is your life.

No one can pay for good and true life because good and true life keeps you going. **Truth is everlasting life so truly live true.**

Lovey did not take our right and rights from us. If he did, we would not have will. He gave us our right to choose good or evil. It's unfortunate that we as humans chose evil then expect him Lovey to come an override our decision after we have sinned reckless and rude. We did not think of our life when we were sinning, but all of a sudden at the final hour we want to be saved.

Michelle

It's November 13, 2015 and I should have been done but dreamt Justin Bieber. Dreamt he was on this high building singing and I was with him. He stopped singing and the massive crowd below began to sing and he just stood there as if he wanted to jump.

Hey this is my weird world.

Leaving this dream alone because it makes no sense to me.

So in all you do in life, truly stay safe and wonderful.

You control your own destiny so control it and stop giving it away to undeserving people.

Michelle

OTHER BOOKS BY MICHELLE JEAN

Blackman Redemption – The Fall of Michelle Jean
Blackman Redemption – After the Fall Apology
Blackman Redemption – World Cry – Christine Lewis
Blackman Redemption
Blackman Redemption – The Rise and Fall of Jamaica
Blackman Redemption – The War of Israel
Blackman Redemption – The Way I Speak to God
Blackman Redemption – A Little Talk With Man
Blackman Redemption – The Den of Thieves
Blackman Redemption – The Death of Jamaica
Blackman Redemption – Happy Mother's Day
Blackman Redemption – The Death of Faith
Blackman Redemption – The War of Religion
Blackman Redemption – The Death of Russia
Blackman Redemption – The Truth
Blackman Redemption – Spiritual War
Blackman Redemption – The Youths
Blackman Redemption – Black Man Where Is Your God?

The New Book of Life
The New Book of Life – A Cry For The Children
The New Book of Life – Judgement
The New Book of Life – Love Bound
The New Book of Life – Me
The New Book of Life – Life

Just One of Those Days
Book Two – Just One of Those Days
Just One of Those Days – Book Three The Way I Feel
Just One of Those Days – Book Four

The Days I Am Weak
Crazy Thoughts – My Book of Sin
Broken
Ode to Mr. Dean Fraser

A Little Little Talk
A Little Little Talk – Book Two

Prayers
My Collective
A Little Talk/A Time For Fun and Play
Simple Poems
Behind The Scars
Songs of Praise And Love

Love Bound
Love Bound – Book Two

Dedication Unto My Kids
More Talk
Saving America From A Woman's Perspective
My Collective the Other Side of Me
My Collective the Dark Side of Me
A Blessed Day
Lose To Win
My Doubtful Days – Book One

My Little Talk With God
My Little Talk With God – Book Two

A Different Mood and World – Thinking

My Nagging Day

My Nagging Day – Book Two
Friday September 13, 2013
My True Love
It Would Be You
My Day

A Little Advice – Talk
1313, 2032, 2132 – The End of Man
Tata

MICHELLE'S BOOK BLOG – BOOKS 1 – 22

My Problem Day
A Better Way
Stay – Adultery and the Weight of Sin – Cleanliness
Message

Let's Talk
Lonely Days – Foundation
A Little Talk With Jamaica – As Long As I Live
Instructions For Death
My Lonely Thoughts
My Lonely Thoughts – Book Two
My Morning Talks – Prayers With God
What A Mess
My Little Book
A Little Word With You
My First Trip of 2015
Black Mother – Mama Africa
Islamic Thought
My California Trip January 2015
My True Devotion by Michelle – Michelle Jean
My Many Questions To God

My Talk
My Talk Book Two
My Talk Book Three – The Rise of Michelle Jean
My Talk Book Four
My Talk Book Five
My Talk Book Six
My Talk Book Seven
My Talk Book Eight – My Depression
My Talk Book Nine – Death
My Talk Book Ten – Wow
My Day – Book Two
My Talk Book Eleven – What About December?
Haven Hill
What About December – Book Two
My Talk Book Twelve – Summary and or Confusion
My Talk Book Thirteen
My Talk Book Fourteen – My Talk With God
My Talk Book Fifteen – My Talk
My Thoughts – Freedom
My Heart to Heart With Lovey – God

Letters to my song and words of praise and truth; My true and unconditional Love; Lovey, Good God and Allelujah